MEXICO

MOSAIC

My beloved, the mountains,

the silent wooded valleys,

strange isles,

resounding rivers,

the sigh of amorous breezes.

St. John of the Cross
Spiritual Canticle

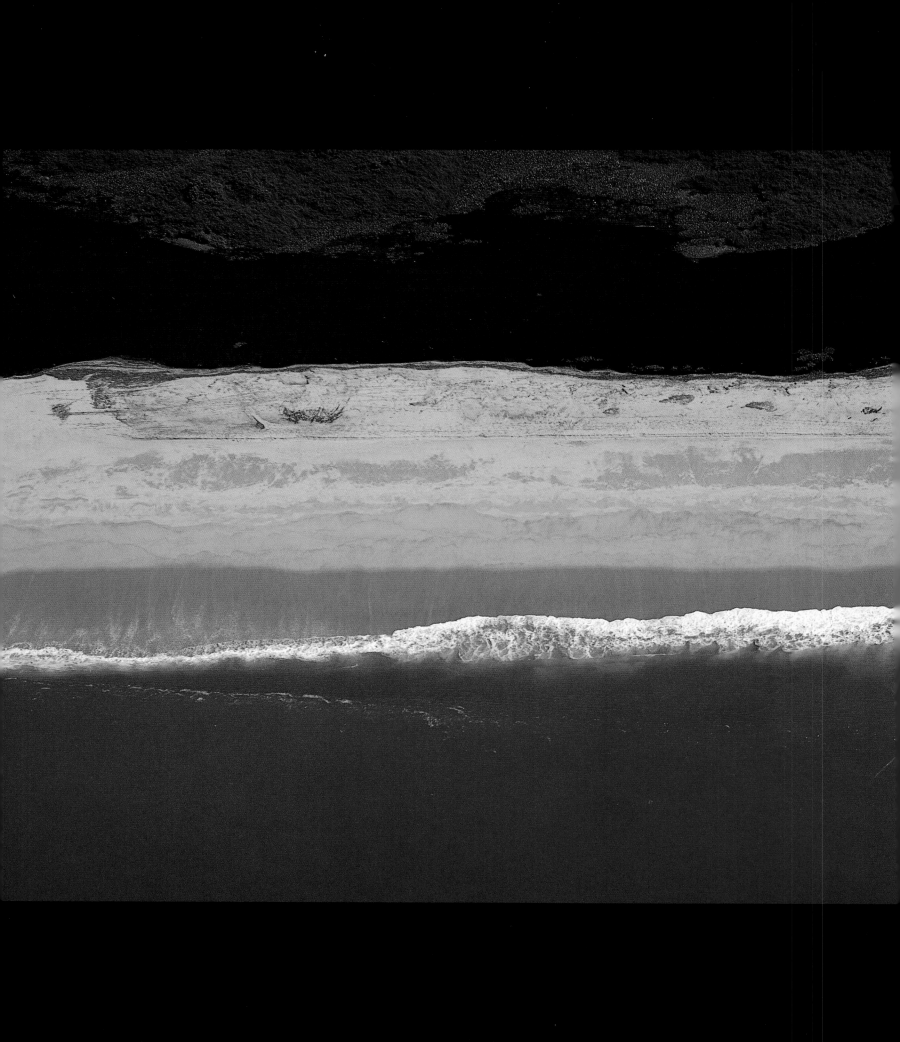

MEXICO
MOSAIC

Photography
MICHAEL CALDERWOOD

Prologue
EDUARDO LIZALDE

Texts
LUIS MIGUEL AGUILAR
ANTONIO DELTORO
VICTOR MANUEL MENDIOLA
VERONICA VOLKOW

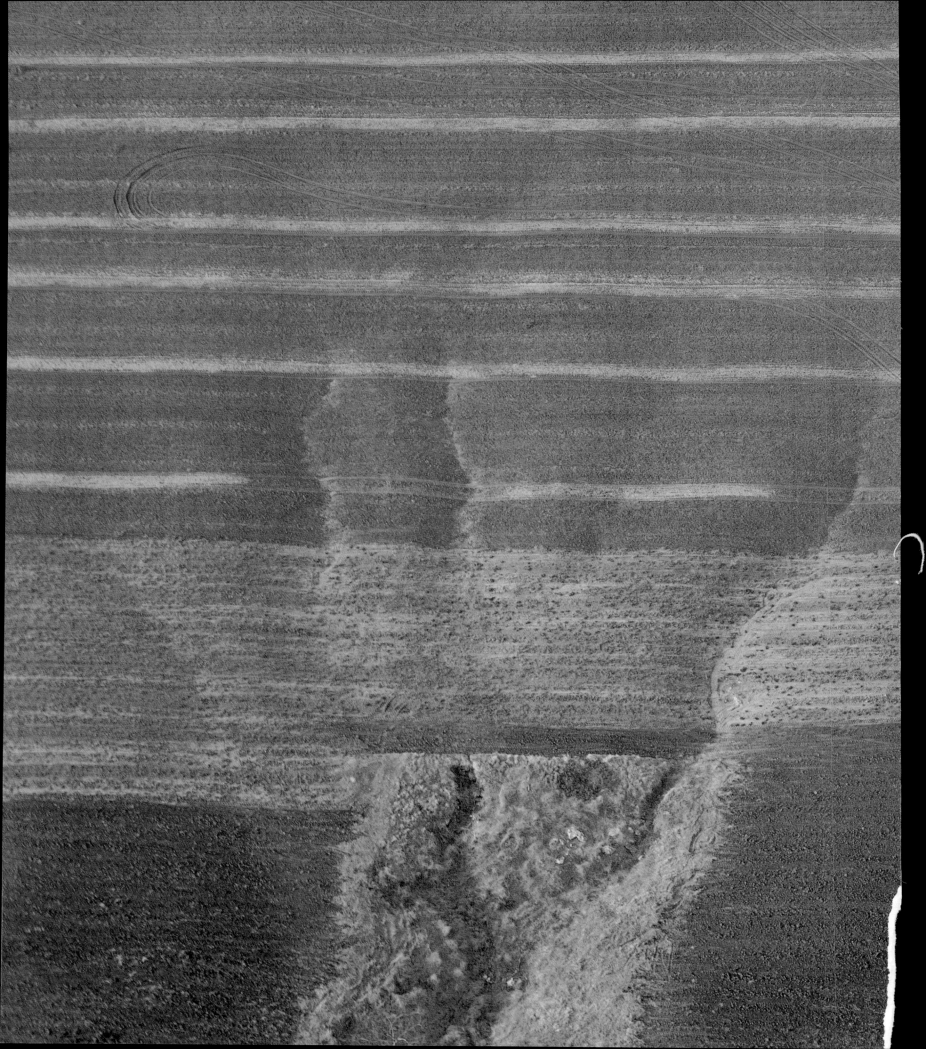

Editorial Direction	John Wiseman
Project Coordinator	Bridget Galsworthy Estavillo
Circulation Consultant	Brian Weiner
Graphic Design	Printt Diseñadores, S.C.
	Eduardo Zapata Gosselín
	Jesús Laveaga Tostado
Translation	John Page
Editorial Coordination	Michael Calderwood

D.R. © Revimundo, S.A. de C.V.
First Edition: 1999
ISBN (9687294086)
Printed in Hong Kong

JACKET: BASALT PRISMS, SANTA MARÍA REGLA, HIDALGO
PAG. 2-3 THE POPOCATEPETL VOLCANO AT DAWN
PAG. 4-5 THE COSTA ALEGRE, JALISCO
PAG. 6 HIBISCUS FLOWER AND MAIZE CULTIVATION, PUEBLA
PAG. 8-9 NEWLY HARVESTED FIELD BY THE COAST OF OAXACA
PAG. 10 THE EAGLE'S NEST, PUNTA DE MITA, NAYARIT

Acknowledgements: MANUEL ARANGO • MARCO BUENINCK • MARCO VINICIO CALDERÓN • ISABEL CAMARGO • ALBA MARGARITA CERVERA LAVAT • SUE CHAPMAN • GRACIELA DE LA VEGA • NIDIA ESQUIVEL DE GALÁN • JENNIKATE ESTAVILLO • JUAN HERNÁNDEZ • WAYNE HILBIG • PETER KLEES • EVA & GREG MAY • MIGUEL MEDINA • PATRICIA MENDOZA • SANTIAGO ORTIZ MONASTERIO • BERTHA RUIZ DE LA CONCHA • FLOR RUVALCABA • ALICIA SCHIEFFER, AND ALL THOSE PILOTS WITHOUT WHOSE SKILL AND PATIENCE THESE PICTURES WOULD NOT HAVE BEEN POSSIBLE. *The photographs reproduced on pages: 51, 86 and 129 appear with the kind permission of the Fundación Xochitla, A.C. The photographs of Punta de Mita are reproduced wirh the kind permission of Dine, S.A. Some of the photographs appearing in the Water and Field chapters were originally published in* México: Tierra Fértil *and* México: Noble Caudal, SARH, 1993-1994.

PREFACE

When I began taking pictures in 1974, there were few indications that photography would become a way of life, even a means of making a living. My conversion to photography leads back directly to my first visit to Mexico. A day or two before boarding the plane out of London, I bought a camera, an austere but workmanlike instrument, mostly made in the USSR. It seemed to match perfectly my own unsophisticated needs: a black box in which to carry a record of my journey, a spontaneous sketchpad of foreign lands to show family and friends on my return. Nothing more.

I was mistaken in both respects. For all its apparent impassivity, the camera developed an unpredictable, and occasionally ruinous, personality, and for myself, I was unable to leave Mexico with little more to show for my travels than an insignificant box of snapshots. In truth, I have never really recovered from that initial encounter (I mean with Mexico, but the camera also played its part), when my life adopted a new and unexpected course.

The photographs selected for this book reflect, I hope, the impression that seeing Mexico made on a young and inexperienced Englishman 25 years ago. Who could resist excitement at the brilliance of light, the vastness of space, and the inconceivably rich panorama of colors, textures and forms? Here is a landscape that feels simultaneously ancient and newborn. The bones of the earth in Mexico lie close beneath its skin, stretching the land taut and vibrant.

THE PAXILHÁ RIVER, CHIAPAS

One evening, on an early trip to the Mixtec region of Oaxaca, the light glancing off rounded ridges made the distant hills crawl, like crimson lizards, along the edge of a valley. A thick knot of black and yellow clouds filled the sky. I took a photograph, no longer to serve the memory, but as an instinctive, emotional response to the drama and beauty of the natural world.

The Russian box is long gone, replaced by something reliably Japanese. Curiously, the motivation for first acquiring a camera still inspires the photography I most enjoy. Many of these photographs are genuine snapshots, made at high speed and often at low altitude, images almost impossible to repeat, and therefore uniquely worthwhile or worthless. There is little time for thought, and the photographer's response to the scene in front of the camera must be immediate and in some way passionate. For all the precision acquired through years of experience, chance still plays a critical part in my photography. The images moving through the viewfinder take root in the memory, but the developed film is always startling, sometimes magical.

Unsurprisingly for a book dedicated to chance, images perhaps thousands of kilometers and years apart when they were made find new meaning when compared on a page or wall. A dialogue is established, and sometimes continued over a sequence of pages. Patterns dominate nature and human activity, and both worlds intersect in unexpected ways. Although structural necessity obliges us to separate the photographs by theme, our real intention is to spin the kaleidoscope from time to time, just to see what might happen.

MICHAEL CALDERWOOD

PROLOGUE

More than fifty years ago, Bernard Berenson wrote that the natural world around us is like a vast text the signs of which we human beings must learn to read. A text, he added, far more complex, for example, than early Chinese writing for it contains an infinitely greater number of signs that require deciphering.

Furthermore, that indecipherable organism of which we as human beings are a part, is an archipelago of territories, seas and skies without frontiers that moves not only outside of our body but into it, for we are also creatures of an organic complexity that posits infinite readings.

Scientists, artists, writers, historians and simple strollers try to read this endless mass of nature by means of the tools provided by all our sensorial abilities to read forms, light, sound, taste, aroma and corporeal qualities perceptible to us. However, it is in the world of art that creators most extensively and directly transfigure, reflect and interpret the immeasurable lucent, spatial and formal variety of nature. However prodigious a musical composition may be in attempting to reproduce the sounds of nature, or inspired a work of literature in describing the phenomena of nature, they can never equal greatness in film, in painting, or photography, as convincing testimony of the visual phenomena peculiar to nature.

Seekers of light, like painters, cinematographers and photographers, know that though all that is perceptible to the eye is light, it is only fully visible when shaped, like the spirit in body, matter, objects and figures, that allow it to flourish in all the chromatic variety of the spectrum.

The seekers of light, who believed that it could only be captured and made art by historically manual media like chalk, brush, pencil, feathers and metal, were wrong. Today we know that any instrument may be used to seek the light, be it mechanical, electronic or pre-historical.

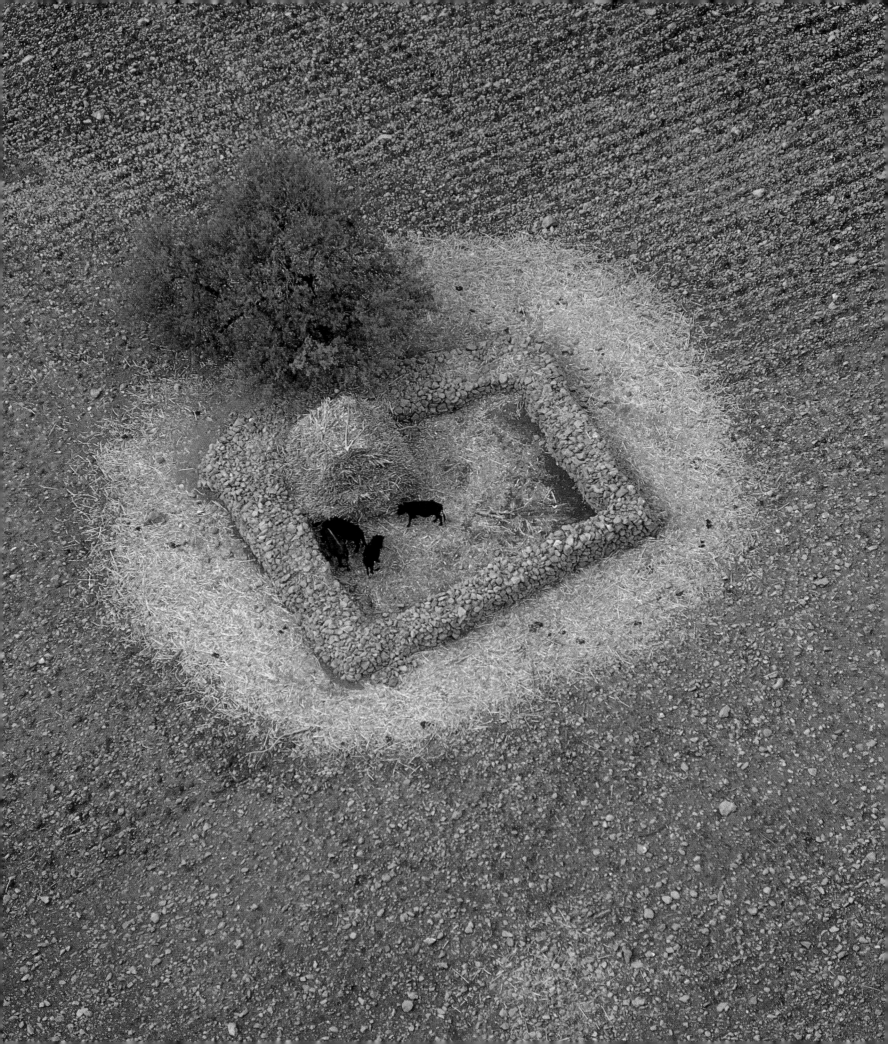

What is important is the eye and the person, the hand behind the computer, the camera, the burin and the sharpened stone.

All artists whether on canvas or other materials work with visions, beings, events and forms of the natural and man-made world, even if it is to repudiate, denature, negate or resist conventional images of that world. It is already a superannuated notion that the works of the most violently imaginative abstractionists in the history of art are like child's play compared to the wealth, variety and dazzling chromatic intensity of the planet's and the cosmos' fertile and unconscious macro and micro organic productions. This, even though "nature imitates art", as Oscar Wilde and others of his epoch insisted in antirealist jocularity.

The already ancient fathers of the criticism of reason and objective idealism clearly understood, as have their philosophical heirs at this end of the century (and the Greeks as well), that natural beauty is only for us who think about it, contemplate it and humanize it. Natural beauty is alienated beauty, to use a Hegelian term. We do not perceive in it the hand of a personal creator. Nor do we see the consciousness of an artisan or artist, an individual self-consciousness, as we remark it precisely in the most insignificant or grandiose work of human creators, be it an arrowhead, a blade, a Gothic church or a pre-Columbian pyramid. Were there a God, an Aristotelian "immovable motor", a creator of the universe, we would in any case (according to these philosophers) not find his imprint, his particular consciousness as creator, artificer in every one of the creatures attributed to him: a condor, a worm or a whale. The most we can expect to find in the beings of creation, according to the Deists, is the anonymous sign of an inexplicable omnipotent divinity. Unalienated objects of ugliness or beauty, rustic furniture, an iron nail, a marble Roman effigy, are the conscious, individual or collective products of mortal, thinking beings and clearly exhibit the imprint, the consciousness of self, of their human creator.

But man, the only attestative creature, who transforms nature, constructs objects, cities, anti-natural places, interplanetary vehicles and, in the process, transforms himself into the worst

enemy of environmental stability, has ultimately humanized the inhuman, alienated beauty of continents, virgin rain forests, seas and inaccessible snow-laden peaks. A hammer, a pair of scissors, simple agricultural implements, have become as human as the creatures of the animal, vegetable and mineral kingdoms, manipulated, changed, domesticated and at times corrupted by the development of industry and society.

Man has over the millennia raised cities of grandiose beauty to barricade himself against the desolate places of the world (hence the Greeks placed architecture on the level of poetry). But it seems that only the personal work of the graphic artist humanizes nature innocently, without touching her, without attacking her, without the least intention of subjugating her or enslaving her. Without even hoping to embellish the insurmountably beautiful, and solely by means of natural acceptance of that grandeur, the graphic artist seeks to produce some other thing that is new and humanly beautiful.

As Veronica Volkow, Luis Miguel Aguilar, Antonio Deltoro and Victor Manuel Mendiola have pointed out from diverse angles in the texts accompanying the several sections of this book, Michael Calderwood's photographs are more than simple testimony to impeccable technique. Calderwood's treatment reveals relief, perspective, grain, texture, depth, and strictly pictorial play of color. We are fortunate that art historians and critics have long abandoned earlier scruples and prejudices against art produced with the assistance of mechanical tools, lenses, and instruments of contemporary technology. The idea that examples of a visual work produced serially belong in the ranks of lesser art and that it is exclusively the original work that may achieve aesthetic value is passing into history.

In the future it may become possible to reproduce the paintings of El Greco or Rembrandt molecularly and serially such that the copy may be indistinguishable from the original. At that point, the cost of the copy will undoubtedly plummet, but its aesthetic value will be the same as in centuries gone by. This is precisely the case of the photographic and cinematographic work of today.

Scientists have been since classical times the most ambitious readers of nature committed to deciphering the mysteries and discovering the principles and laws of life, the universe and the world. Artists and philosophers of art, though the latter sought to find principles and precepts universally applicable to all human endeavor, finally understood that the poetic task (in the largest sense of the term), could not be equal to that of the gods. Overwhelmed by the incon- ceivable, immense and aweinspiring reality of creation, they had to settle for following in its steps, imitating it and recreating it, emulating it in human terms if that were possible. It is to this that Aristotle alludes, among other things, with his idea of mimesis.

In the most dogged periods of realist painting and photography of centuries past and present, those who were fascinated by their ambition to bring the living, whole, exact image of a city

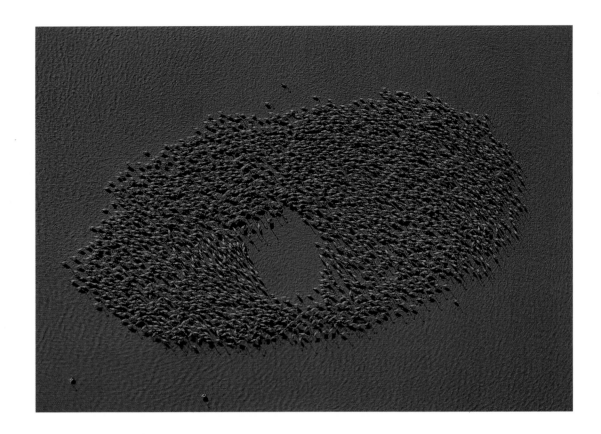

East or West, a storm on the high seas, a battle between ships under sail, had no recourse but to synthesize the phenomenon. They had to materialize the real and unrepeatable emotion by falling back on symbolic, diminished and ultimately frustrating reproduction on canvas or animated film. It has happened to all of us no matter how clear the impression of reality and beauty delivered in paintings, on film or in photographs of the piazza San Marco, the Great Wall or the Acropolis. All become miserable postal cards and yellowed family memorabilia when we ourselves stand before these portents and see them with our own eyes.

The same has occurred with substances, liquids, solid elements of the natural world; in order not to emulate the gods, man has erected impossible, miraculous, anti-natural urban works. He has subdued rivers, constructed inorganic creatures and violated original genetic engineering.

A FLOCK OF FLAMINGOS FEEDS IN THE SHALLOW WATERS OF THE CELESTÚN LAGOON, YUCATAN

Similarly, from ancient times he discovered that the biological cycle of the vegetable kingdom could serve him and give him the materials to create the peculiarly human art of gardening (compared by Kant to the most exalted forms of art), a phenomenon known to all civilizations.

Michael Calderwood, master photographer, knows how to dispose and remodel the visual matter of Mexican nature without repeating the works of our great landscape artists whether they worked with brush or lens. He offers us these flashes of denuded and powerful beauty, as they do not appear anywhere but to the rigor of his eye, though they are everywhere in our limitless world.

EDUARDO LIZALDE

SEA

An Abyss Without Demons

There are two seas: the sea and the sea created by art. Sometimes they are indistinguishable. Do we see the sea, or *the sea*? Are we looking at a tempest or a painting by Turner? Are we looking at a distant, almost uniform and undulating mass of water or a panther skin by Valéry? The sea is a modern invention. To have asked the ancients about its beauty would have been like asking us today about the beauty of some factory or dangerous highway. "The sea is of the century", said St. Augustine, meaning thereby that it was of "this world". In other words, it was an element subject to evil, sin, and composed of the abyss and demons. It has cost the sea considerable effort to come by the reputation for beauty that it enjoys today among us. Even the idea of recreation, of seaside bathing, is a product of the late 18th century.

Like the joyful or enjoyable fear of the sea, the artistic notion of the sea, perhaps because it is also terrifying, is sublime. It is only recently that the sea has been treated as a matter of artistic deliberation. It was only in the 19th century that the aesthete John Ruskin posited the sea as an element whose complexity was its only justification in art: "To paint water in all its perfection is as impossible as painting the soul". The sea has become an artistic, literary reference even when we are confronting it. Or perhaps it is the other way around, and we become cleansed of literature and cleansed of *the sea* every time we come in contact with the sea, though that is unlikely. The more we seek *the sea*, the more likely we are to find it. Perhaps Oscar Wilde put an end to nature, to the romantic idea of nature –in itself a very anti-natural idea– when he said that nature tends to imitate art. We are, ultimately, the sea: half sea and half art about the sea.

But the moment a wave knocks us down we remember that the second half is preferable to the

first. The modern invention of the sea refers to an "aesthetic" of the sea. That, however, does

not mean that only in modern times has humanity made art of it. On the contrary, any human

contact with the sea, however primal, makes it artistic. I am reminded for example of a word

referring to the sea that is, or was, a work of art in itself and that today is used only routinely

in weather reports: the word hurricane, *ouragan*, in French. This word is actually ancient

Mayan, created out of knowledge of the adversity of the sea. It is a word composed of *hurah*

which in Mayan means wind, and *kahn*, serpent. Serpent of the wind. It is not only a painting

made of words, it is a painting that speaks or sounds. If we take the phonetic of *hurah* as

actually *huuurah*, we already have the sound of the wind. If we take the phonetic *kahn* as a kind of stroke or blow, like a serpent on the attack, we have a sophisticated work of art that was not supposed to be that, but rather to describe a maritime phenomenon.

Humanity has always granted intent to the sea. We lend the modern sea artistic intent. A ship run aground in the nineteen-fifties on reefs in the Mexican Caribbean is today, in our eyes, a work of art composed of the strange fusion of the skeletal remains of ship and coral, the latter having decided to incorporate the former into its movements and give it life. The sea not only as "natural" sculptor, carver of rocks and molder of coastlines, but as artist capable of combining and fusing dissimilar materials in the process of 20th century creation.

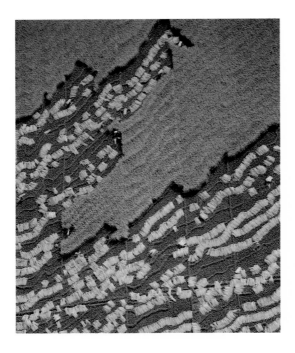

Similarly, once on a ship crossing the same Mexican Caribbean, I had the feeling that maritime art and its combination of colors would, in the long run, make me sweat blue. No artist could pull that off in color. Until I realized that the pale blue on my right, to one side of the ship, was due solely to the fact that the sea's depth at that point was only a meter and a half. On my left, on the other side of the ship, deep blue. The weight of that blue on my eyes was due to some three hundred and fifty fathoms of pre-human, unbearable, geological depth: the vertigo, in spite of the water, of an abyss. This was an abyss without demons, contrary to St. Augustine's, but an abyss no less.

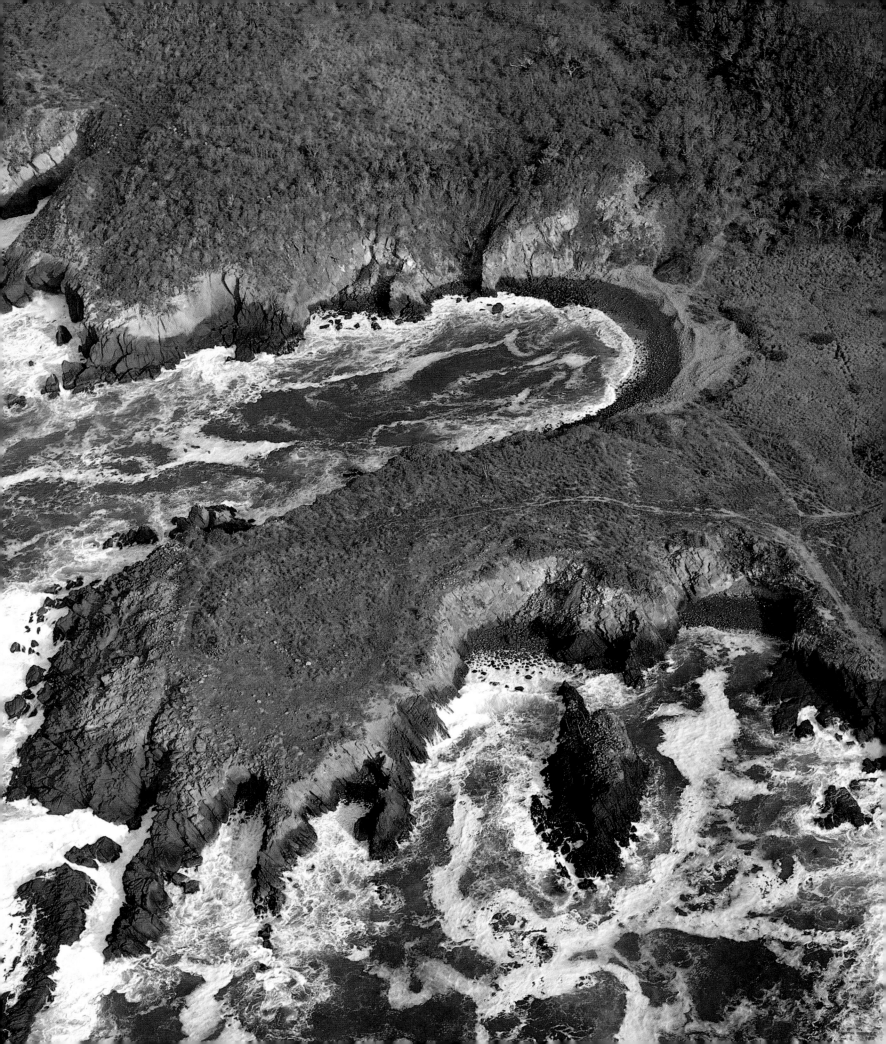

But, did I not feel this an aesthetic experience? Did I not include literature in my own vertigo? We don't believe in the sea. We believe, rather, that its ultimate truth is an artistic truth. It is a paradox that the history of the art of the sea has not so much consisted in "humanizing" it as in making it inhuman. In distancing it from us so that it will not devastate us but will, ultimately, be tranquilized and tranquilize us so that we can withstand its overpowering proximity. If we distance the sea, we bring it closer. We make it almost understandable. It is in this "almost" that the emotion of the sea lies, the aesthetic revelation that makes us return to it, that which we recognize as its own works of art and works of art about the sea. The sea is an aesthetic "almost". Every time we get the feeling that now we have it, it escapes us again. Into the distance or into another blue or into another orange sunset or who knows where. Toward ourselves? Once the moderns discovered the sea, once art brought us close to it, and distanced us from it, the sea became for us a constant invention. This invention has lent the sea artistic capacity unbeknownst to the sea itself. Without our gaze, without our words the sea would be only a giant capable of a few monotonous rhythms and a single repetitive obsession: the sea itself.

Part of our work on this earth consists in reinventing the sea or in discovering how it may reinvent itself. The sea knows not that it is pictorial or sculptural art, nor that it is history and even less, (despite what is said about it) music, unless we make it known to the sea. How shall we reinvent the sea? By touching it again and again, though we know that in doing so we approach it only momentarily and send it away momentarily. In other words, we make it imminent and our own only to leave it irremediably intact, interminable, again rejecting art and human comprehension. All we can make is an almost: almost the sea, almost a secret, almost a revelation, almost ourselves.

The latest reinvention of the sea has undoubtedly to do with the "aerial" sea, that is, the sea seen by the eyes of the artist, from on high. The aerial eye, the artistic moment of surprising the sea from great altitude –far away and very close, neither very high nor very low– is a reinvention that would be impossible without the 20th century. There will be other reinventions of the sea. The novelty of this reinvention is that in it the sea is unaware that it is an artist until it can see itself from on high. The sea already knew, for example, that it was romantic, a sublime spirit, sweeping aside all moral strictures with great aspirations, with an immense "I". It also knew that it was a great novelist. All subjects, situations and characters were there in it.

It knew that it was the greatest of historians, not simply a witness to all events but master of invaluable documents. The sea, today, sees itself and lets us see it in this photographic art as it is seen by the divinity. Or better than the divinity, as a child would see it, as if the sea looked at itself with the eyes of a child, which is after all the aspiration of all divinity and of all art, to return to the beginning, see itself for the first time, reinvent itself. Surprised from great altitudes, the sea is surprised by its taste for play, for play that, as we know, is neither capricious nor arbitrary, but careful and disciplined. From great altitudes the sea feels like playing with the sea and the coastline, like making models and putting in little pieces of plastic to its satisfaction.

John Keats says that a poet is lost if he has lost his innocence. The sea would say the same from high up: these labors, these designs to scale, these games with watercolors, moss, sand and plasticine, these miniatures are the proof of my constant reinvention. Do not call me old, tired or terminated. I continue to create because I have not lost my innocence.

LUIS MIGUEL AGUILAR

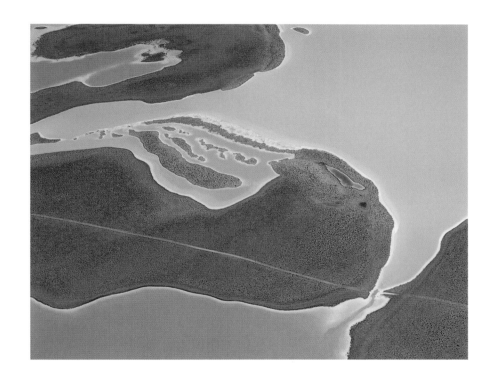

PAG.48 SUNSET AT PUNTA DE MITA, NAYARIT
PAG.49 THE IMPERCEPTIBLE LINE DIVIDING LAND AND SEA, SINALOA

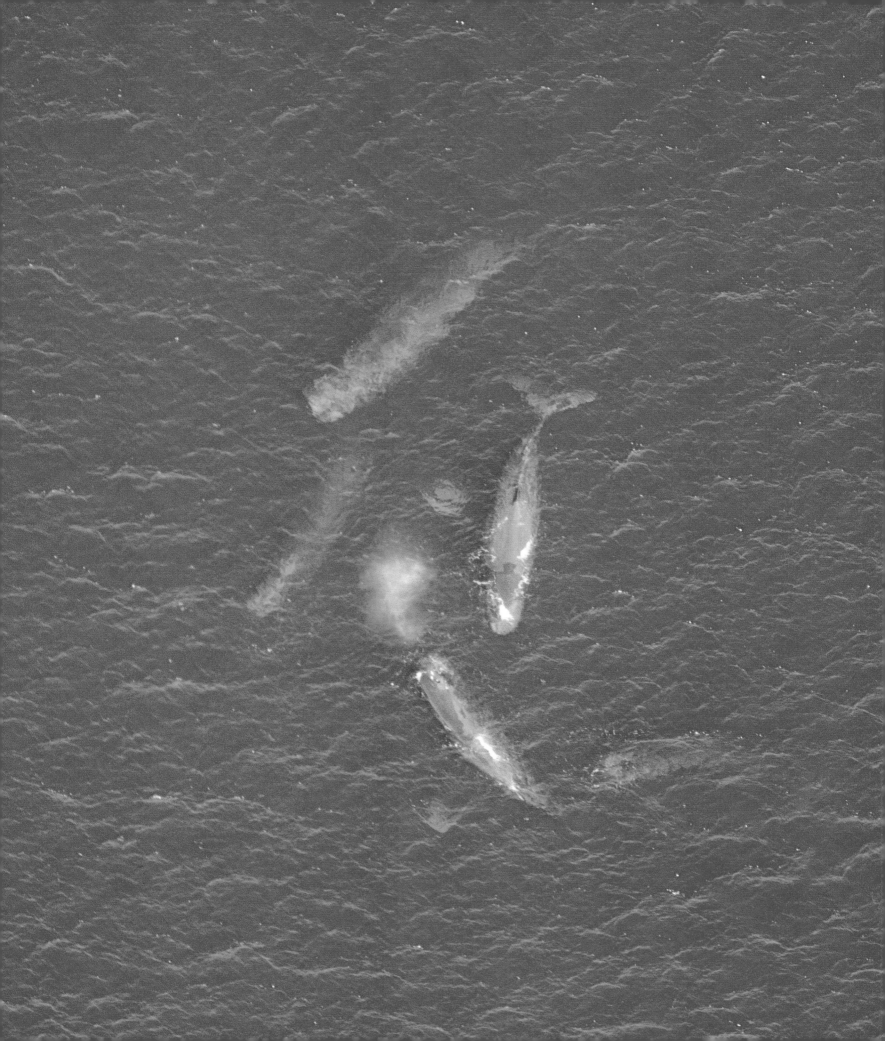

PAG. 58 THE SHALLOW INLAND LAGOONS AT CELESTUN, YUCATAN / PAG. 59 MANGROVE ENTRANCE TO THE NICHUPTE LAGOON, CANCUN

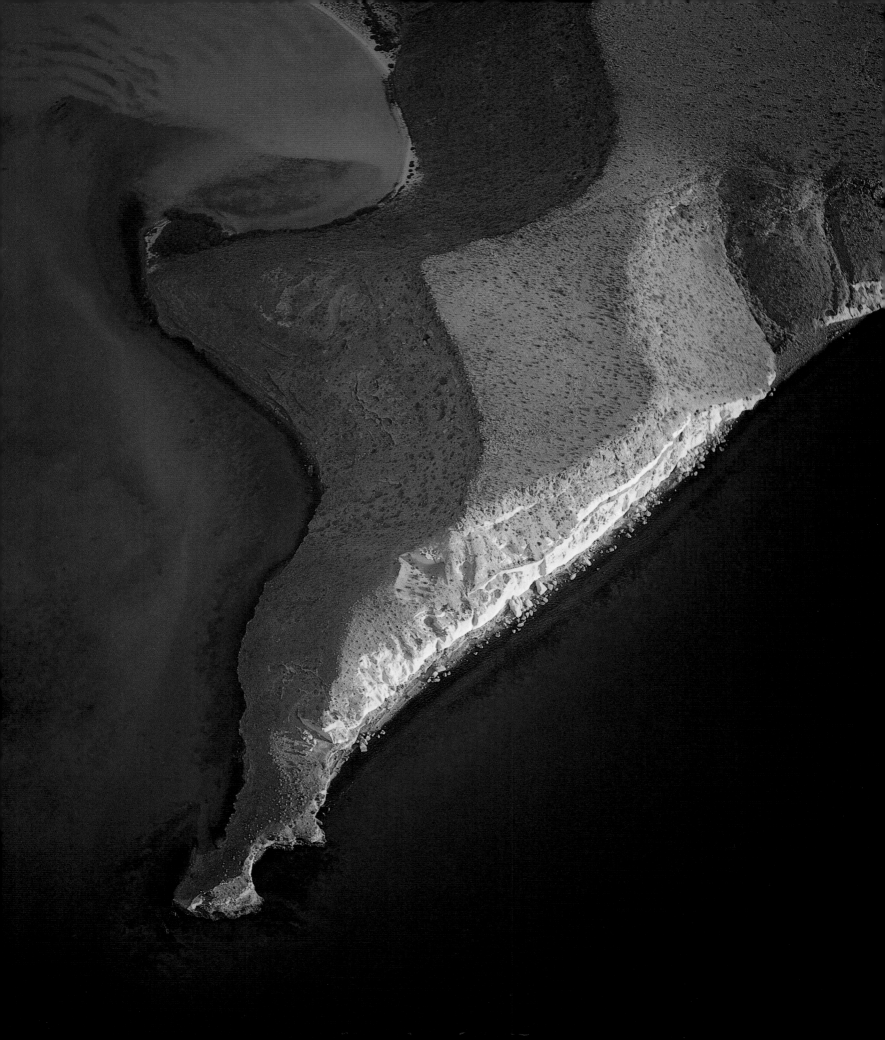

THE SEA,
CARVER OF ROCKS,
MOLDER OF COASTLINES

LAND

THE KINGDOM OF SOLITARY OPEN AIR

These images are instants, to quote Luis Cernuda, by means of which we glimpse *A time whose rhythm recalls not that poor,*

long and vast rhythm of our short,

weak human time.

From the air we can apprehend immense expanses but also, in a privileged instant, a touch of eternity. Those who dominate the air, inhabit the encompassing atmosphere, find themselves like the gods in a vaster time. In cities our eyes are constrained by walls. Our horizon is restricted. Necessity and haste reduce us to fragmented and straitened time. Time in the mountains and the forests is a time as great as the space they occupy. Sedentary and terrestrial, we reach that time through the eyes of a bird.

These images capture the magnificent repertoire of forms in nature, from the obelisk and the pyramid to abstract art. They reveal to us that these forms were present before we existed, indifferent, of course, to the history of art but available to imagination and thought.

Our country, our geography, have been fields of exploration in which these fragments that condense all the aesthetic wealth of the earthly crust were found. Although they lie beneath Mexican skies they are able to move and amaze all who regard them.

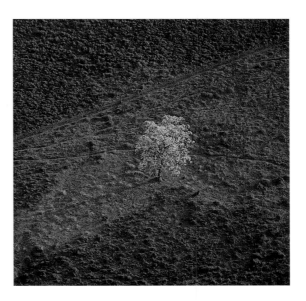

The aerial view offers us what was previously available only to shamans and eagles and it provides us in our waking hours with what we could only see before in our dreams. In these images, reality seems often to overflow and equal the purest and most elevated aesthetic dreams, farthest from any material or territorial reference. The eye doubts. Where am I, what is it that I see? One step further and nature becomes abstract, universal; a rock, a cactus, clouds and mountains sing the same tune or speak the same language. We know not if the eye that looks at us from below, an oasis of white sand and opalescent colors, is in Campeche or Sinaloa. No matter.

All we wish is to share with our lover for at least an instant its beauty and regard the immensity of the sky from within it.

In these photographs there are views without a scrap of sky that are no less aerial than the others. They are absolute in their verticality and provide us, without vertigo, the eyes of a bird. Diving or gliding in minute exploration. In these vistas where the solid occupies all of space, sight sometimes acquires the quality of touch and we can feel the soft undulations of ground and the hardness of rock. In most of these images the air is not only omnipresent, cutting out and outlining things, but in an almost literal sense it is the terrain upon which the photographer

FARM SURROUNDED BY AGAVE FIELDS, THE HIGHLANDS OF JALISCO

stands to take his pictures. It is the shore from which he contemplates this other shore below

on which we live and from which we cast our eye. The flying eye claims a view that

complements that of the terrestrial observer. His eyes are like those of a bird seeking neither

prey nor nest here below but the beauty of forests and mountains. He who looks in this way

sees the reverse of the terrestrial observer, it is he who moves and what he sees is at rest.

Perhaps this is what causes him to approach a vaster time.

From this point of view we witness a dance in which clouds and mountains, the fleeting and

the eternal, gaseous and solid, dance to the same tune. It is from here that clouds fall but not

as drops, as in rain, but caressing and sliding like waterfalls. Watching the open air from above, the eye lends spirit to the world below. It does so in the same way as a painting by El Greco, in which the stony mass of Toledo seems to fly. The eye does not confront the solid in the way that an architect or a sculptor does, but rather like a painter, extracting more than texture or matter from things, but in everything finding design and music. It feels no fatigue in the experience of the sierra but rather in the dance of the peaks. Thus the eye, more than a working eye, the vacationing eye, mixes the worlds of light and gravity, ascent and descent, to obtain the fruits which are, in spite of their lightness, as much the children of crystallization as of evaporation, equally indebted to earth and air.

The landscapes we see here are the kingdom of solitary open air. These are virgin lands that seem to be colonized only by the eyes of the dreamers of clouds and by the vigilant eyes of eagles. They seem to be viewed by a being for whom contemplation is prior to identification, by an eye that is pure, primal, open, surprised, that first alights and then feels; then defines, recognizes and recalls. These images are pure and need no recognition to be enjoyed. A cascade of clouds, of water is, for this spirit two forms of the same feeling, the same pleasure, the same joy.

From above, things seem pacified but not tame, sometimes drowsy, somnolent, but alive and powerful. Curiously, these vistas do not provoke fear or vertigo in the viewer. On the contrary, we glide in silent admiration of the spectacle, metamorphosed into birds. Like birds we feel no vertigo, just as there is no bird that does not take the air for its homeland.

Thanks to these images, we may take it for granted that the atmosphere is our home and that the valleys and the mountains of Mexico are ours. We can also breathe better, loosening a little the hold of gravity and setting out on our aesthetic adventures of flight. The eye that contemplates these landscapes rises not like the astronaut to become independent of the force of gravity and to flee the earth, but out of love for the earth, to observe it.

ANTONIO DELTORO

THE ALTAR DESERT AND THE PINACATE RESERVE, SONORA

PAG.86 FUMAROLAS WITHIN THE CRATER OF THE EL CHICHONAL VOLCANO, CHIAPAS
PAG.87 POPOCATEPETL AFTER A WINTER SNOWSTORM

TWO FORMS
OF THE SAME FEELING,
THE SAME PLEASURE,
THE SAME JOY

PAG.92 THE VALLEY OF CUICATLAN, OAXACA / PAG.93 ERODED HILLSIDES, YANHUITLAN, OAXACA
PAG.94-95 THE SIERRA MADRE ORIENTAL, NUEVO LEÓN

92 | 93

PAG.96 NOPAL CACTUS FIELDS, FLORES MAGON, DURANGO / PAG.97 SIERRA EL TESORERO, NUEVO LEÓN

A DANCE IN WHICH
THE CLOUDS AND THE MOUNTAINS
DANCE TO THE SAME TUNE

FIELD

THE LINES OF HUMAN COMPOSITION

For centuries we walked or were drawn by ox or carried by nag. By those measures things hardly moved, while at the pace of a thoroughbred horse or camel, a race ended in the blink of an eye and the thrill or terror of mounted warfare was quickly over. Pursuit of a thief or flight from danger at the top speed of a mustang could not surpass the physical capacity of the animal itself. Flying on the wings or in the claws of a fantastic bird, as does Sinbad in the Arabian Nights, was only a dream.

At the speed of the machine we enter mobile immobility. At 60, 150 or 800 kilometers per hour, we experience a paradox: we move without moving. The vertiginous speed of the machine shares our repose with it. Trees, hills, clouds pass one after another but we remain immutable. We breathe calmly, our pulse normal.

The sense of peace inside the machine is discrete, pleasurable. We cross our legs, our arms, close our eyes or open them to see the vanishing landscape. Our head falls from one side to the other and our thoughts hop and skip in that equilibrium in which stillness and movement establish an invisible boundary. A change of speed reminds us that this equilibrium may disappear. Inertia shakes our contentment out of its comfort, throwing us forward or back. It wakes us, stirs our drowsiness or breaks our concentration, shaking, even thumping us.

The speed of the machine makes us otherwise. It shrinks space, brings closer what we want and distances us from what we don't want. Speed is more and more like thought: an instantaneous succession of images joined in one dazzling picture.

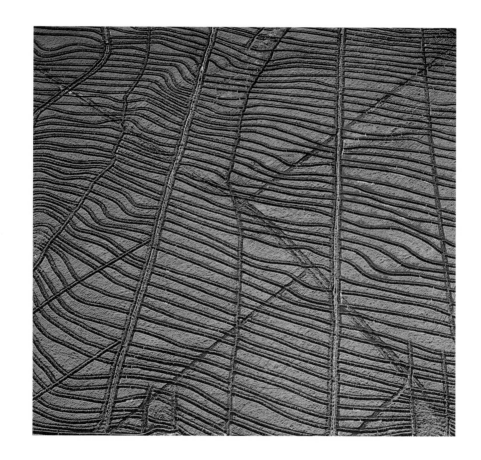

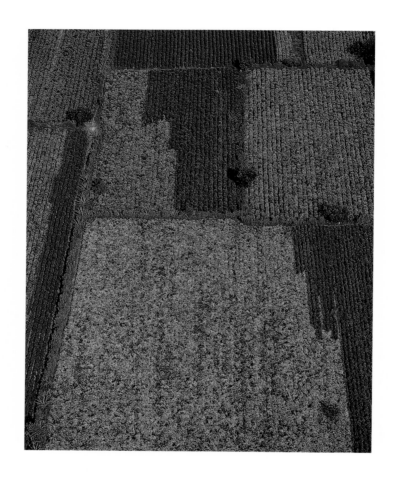

Photographs taken at speed, and particularly the speed of flight, produce images which express that contrary double quality of making us move without moving. We rise in a machine that is not of time but of movement/stillness. The nature we view is suspended in flight. There is only the dimension of altitude. Things (a bridge, a garden, a village, a reservoir) produce an unexpected sensation of rising/falling speed. The significance lies in the discovery of an unusual fact: the spontaneous appearance of nature contrasting with the orderly outlines of human activity.

The crests and depths of a canyon develop spontaneously: they twist unexpectedly and plunge out of control. The shapes of great accumulations of stone and dust and water reveal dramatic energy suggesting that nature's best efforts are turned to crushing, cutting, breaking and melting. But, when we look at the dense green lines of a cornfield or the grid of an orchard we think that for his survival man has fragmented the world to extract pure and invisible figures like the dot, the line and the plane, from the folds of earth and sky.

Seeing the reality we have created from the perspective of an airplane, we realize that man not only conceives abstract design but, striving to satisfy the necessities of life, creates geometry while laying out his gardens. From the sky, the signs of labor in the earth, reticulated forests, fields of flowers and vegetables, reveal order, design and therefore art, an aesthetic. Before, in a world measured by the foot and the horse, any man could climb a mountain and from there see clearly the order of cultivation, but not the clean lines of human composition.

Before the age of the machine the eye was prisoner to the foot. Now, under the headlong dominion of speed, we see with our own eyes that as we scratch the earth, though we sometimes destroy it, we often make it beautiful.

VICTOR MANUEL MENDIOLA

By scratching the earth,
we may destroy it
or make it more beautiful

PAG.128 FIELDS OF SUGAR CANE, MORELOS / PAG.129 MAIZE FIELDS IN THE TARAHUMARA SIERRA, CHIHUAHUA

PAG.132 A HERD OF CATTLE, COAHUILA / PAG.133 ABANDONED IRRIGATION FIELD SYSTEMS, NUEVO LEON
PAG.134-135 PALM PLANTATIONS FOR OIL EXTRACTION, COLIMA
PAG.136-137 LA GAVIA RANCH, STATE OF MEXICO

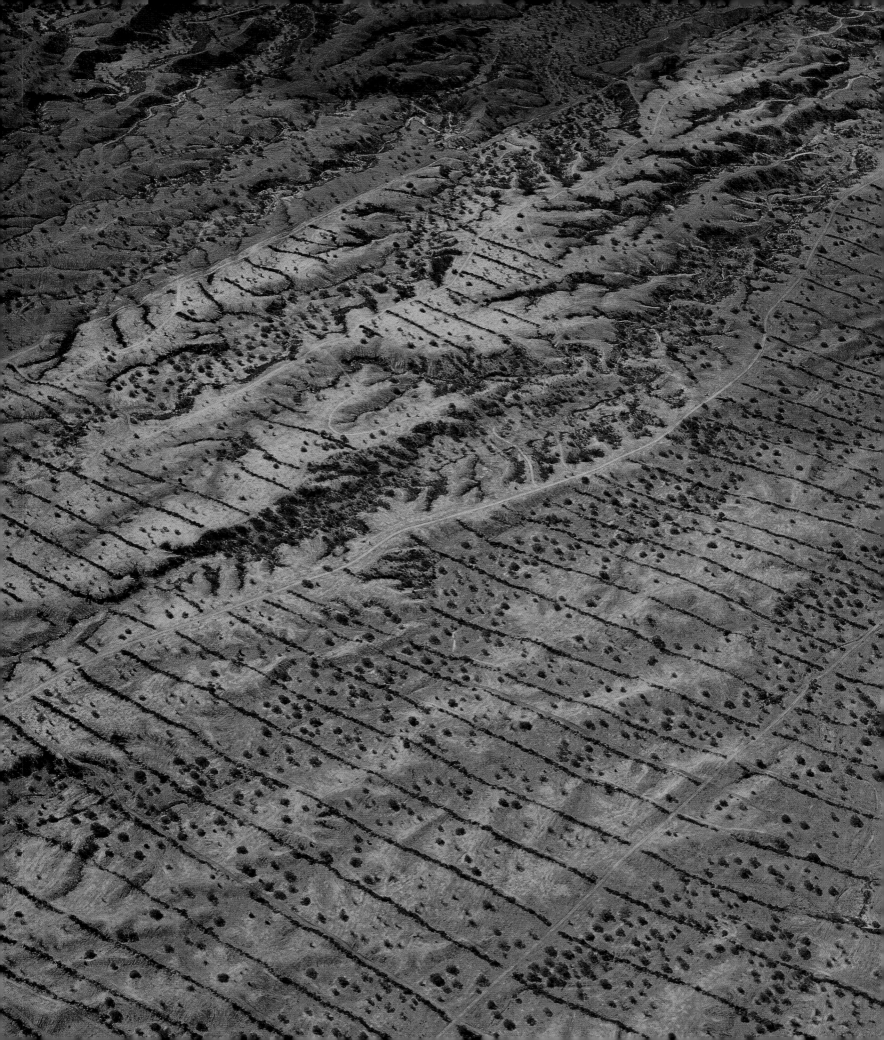

WATER

THE MIRROR AND THE BRIDGE

A rushing river, its waterfall cascading from a cliff, introduces a story, a narrative, a silken moon-colored filament that binds trees and stones and defines an abyss. A river is being written in the valley. Nothing resembles language like a river. Its undulant manuscript, its interminable fricative phonemes advance, write, sing, accompany us along the way. A river writes a story among the mountains, the narrative of something to come, the memory of what was.

Of all that has body, water is the closest to invisible. Restrained by the geography of solids, it always borders a beach, a ship, a port, a glass. Thus does it allow itself to be domesticated by forms, within their molds, never entirely yielding its unharnessed self. We see it reach the horizon's infinity, escape from any crack or, hypnotized by its inner self, examine its own abysmal transparency. All water is, somehow, a cataract, the pellucid muscle of displacement.

It is as if water were by itself a bridge or a boat reaching out to unknown destinations. In mythology one reaches the other side of death by crossing a river or a lake. Water is the mediator of other dimensions, it leads to the thresholds of what drowns in the invisible.

It explores all forms, yet is none of them, a transparent serpent that from birth learns to search all riverbeds. It is like a sun that radiates, not as light, but as liquid.

Although water extends an invitation to a journey, as a port of embarkation, in a forest or mountain setting it is above all a point of gathering, of withdrawal, of arrival. It falls toward itself and teases the landscape into the curves of its riverbed, treasuring its emeralds and intense indigos, retailing its liquid jewels. Water opens another dimension that does not exist in space, folded into itself it creates an inner world.

Gaston Bachelard writes that every pool is an eye for the poetry of landscape. The mirror in which Narcissus admires himself reflects the landscape around him. Nature radiates its splendor in the pool, exhibits its beauty in the mirror. The landscape becomes a spring of unbelievable greens, a source of itself. Around a pool, trees are more than bodies, they are radiant beings.

But water is never an external eye, it is the eye through which things look and are seen. Trees, stones, skies make of the pool their eye. Every image here is an eye, just as every eye is in turn an image. The pool is an eye-object, an eye in search of a subject to admire and to be admired by.

To the ancient Mexicans it was jade not gold that was precious, because of its resemblance to natural beauty. The jade of the forest's water is a symbol of growth, the green fuse that ignites the trees and sets off the explosion of the tropics.

There is always suspense around a lake, a holding of the breath in the presence of grandeur. In this amazed suspense images are immobilized, extracted from the future, as if formed in the surface in which they are fixed. We yearn for that moment, we want it to endure, to become eternal. We wish the landscape would become ours. The photographic image becomes part of the motion of internalization, almost a memory. It is through beauty that the soul wishes to possess the world. It is through beauty that we fall in love, that we desire the more to be.

The love of poets is like water. The world not only contemplates itself in that liquid reflection, as Bachelard points out, but beautifies itself, idealizes itself, aspires to a growing perfection. It is an unfinished image that is always caught in the water's reflection, seeking to become sharper, richer, more refined.

Edgar Allan Poe dreamt of building an absolutely perfect landscape in the water's reflection.

It was thus that in the Domain of Arnheim he attempted to pursue the motto that art perfects

nature. Only the reflected landscape achieves the ambitious dream.

The world impressed in the water's reflection has brought other poets close to a view of paradise. The water's reflection would be like the original Eden, the starting point. The aquatic reflection is not a copy, but on the contrary, an archetype. That paradise is a beginning, a source of the world.

For Heraclitus, that darkness, that same water, its images entirely washed away, was what caused the universe to spring forth, the ark, the essence of origin. For him, the river was one of the privileged metaphors of time and especially of change.

But the river speaks not of the circular time of the cosmos, but the passing of man in time. A river is an irreversible progression, like a life. Within this vastness of nothing, the river is not content with just being. It must seek, seek itself, follow a destiny, change, be unrepeatable.

Nothing accompanies the traveler like a river. It is a friendly presence, almost intimate in the happy solitude of travel, that resounding solitude that reflects, talks to itself as it faces the journey's surprises. Every river is a path, and every path knows its surroundings even as it looks within itself. Therefore, every path must speak, demanding inner growth.

VERÓNICA VOLKOW

PAG.152 MONARCH BUTTERFLIES, CHINCUA, MICHOACAN / PAG.153 THE AGUA AZUL CASCADES, CHIAPAS

EVERY POOL IS
AN EYE FOR THE
POETRY OF LANDSCAPE

AGRICULTURAL DAM IN THE STATE OF MEXICO

To the ancient Mexicans
it was jade, not gold,
that was precious